ENGLISH LANDSCAPE GARDENS

JOHN CURTIS

Text by Richard Ashby

SALMON

INTRODUCTION

It has been said that the landscape garden is England's greatest contribution to the arts. Until the early 18th century gardens tended to be influenced by formal French styles. The political reaction to the French influence at court, a classical education, the 'Grand Tour' and the discovery of the 'Arcadian' landscapes of artists such as Claude Lorrain and Nicolas Poussin, along with a growing appreciation of nature, and especially nature tamed, all led to the development of a new style of garden. Now the gardener worked with, rather than against, nature. In addition, gardens were planned to evoke feelings, so that 'picturesque' or 'awful' elements would be introduced, with temples, grottos, caves and chasms, to enliven visitors as they made their tour. Two literary men, Joseph Adison, the editor of 18th century journal 'The Spectator', and Alexander Pope, the poet, were the first to expound this new theory. Stephen Switzer was the first to turn their ideas into practice. He was followed by 'Capability' Brown, Humphry Repton and many others, who made a lasting impact on the English idea of what a great garden should be. Although the principles were shared by the garden designers the outcomes were often very different. Changes in fashion and economic circumstances have led to the destruction of many fine gardens, but a large number survive and many have been restored. A visit to one is an experience to be savoured.

Stowe Landscape Gardens, *Buckinghamshire*

CIRENCESTER PARK, *Gloucestershire*

Cirencester Park harks back to the earlier ideas of more formal design. In collaboration with his friend Alexander Pope, who had a very influential garden at Twickenham, Lord Bathurst planted thousands of trees creating a vast forest. Through this he cut ten radiating avenues or 'rides' of which the longest, at five miles, is centred on the tower of Cirencester parish church.

CROOME PARK, *Worcestershire*

It is said that Lancelot Brown got his nickname 'Capability' from his response to an enquiring landowner that his grounds had 'capabilities of improvement'. His trade mark was the planting of native trees in strategically placed groups, or 'clumps', and he was a master with water. Croome was the first estate where the plan is Brown's own and it made his name. He was ruthless in his improvements, draining the marshy land for the 'Pleasure Ground', creating a vast lake, sweeping away the village and rebuilding the church so that its tower crowned the view from the house. His work was much appreciated by his employer, the 6th Earl of Coventry, who erected a monument in his honour.

CASTLE HOWARD, *North Yorkshire*

The garden at Castle Howard is hardly a garden at all. Rather it is a landscape where the planting of trees and the placing of buildings has created a vast picture. No one who has seen the television series 'Brideshead Revisited' will forget the funeral procession of Lord Marchmain as it wound its way across the bridge here to the mausoleum on the far side of the shallow valley. Lord Carlisle's architect, Sir John Vanbrugh, was responsible for the overall conception of the garden design, which took some 40 years to bring to fruition. He worked with another famous architect, Nicholas Hawksmoor, who designed a temple as well as the mausoleum to create what is recognised to be the first great English garden in this new style.

HAWKSTONE PARK, *Shropshire*

Hawkstone evokes the scenery of Switzerland. The great park contains an outcrop of sandstone some 500ft above the valley through which nature has driven a great chasm. Generations of the Hill family moulded this terrain into a fantastic landscape. Visitors would walk through great clefts in the rock, passing a grotto, precipice, cave, hermitage (originally with a live hermit) across a Swiss bridge and through a rock arch. The gardens became extremely well known in the 18th century, attracting many visitors who would stay for two or three days in a local inn especially fitted up for them. Bankruptcy led to the park being sold piecemeal and the walks became overgrown. Happily, though, much has been restored and visitors are again able to experience this magical landscape.

STOURHEAD, *Wiltshire*

The remarkable garden at Stourhead was designed by Henry Hoare II, called 'the Magnificent', a prosperous London banker, and it is explicitly modelled on the paintings of Poussin. The shorter walk around the lake takes the visitor through groves of trees, past a Gothic cottage and temples and through this grotto with its reclining nymph. The more energetic can explore the wider landscape including Alfred's Tower, built to commemorate the accession of George III. It was hit by an American aircraft in World War II but has since been repaired.

CHISWICK HOUSE, *London*

William Kent trained in Rome as a painter. While there he came across the paintings of Claude Lorrain and Poussin with their idealised landscapes. In 1716, whilst on the 'Grand Tour', he met Lord Burlington who became his patron and friend and in whose family he lived for 30 years. Burlington had already begun his garden at Chiswick but he invited Kent to help him improve it. Here Kent was able to put into practice his principle that 'all nature is a garden' and that it was the duty of the gardener to treat nature like the canvas of the painter and create the picturesque landscape. The Roman influence is prominent and the garden contains the earliest English garden temples.

PAINSWICK ROCOCO GARDEN, *Gloucestershire*

'Rococo' is an architectural style characterised by lightness, extravagance, elegance and flamboyance. Gardens in the rococo style are dotted with incongruous and playful buildings of contrasting styles. There is an element of this in many 18th century gardens, but it reaches its most perfect form here at Painswick which is also notable for its carpets of snowdrops in the early spring.

PAINSHILL PARK, *Surrey*

Painshill Park has been described as 'one of the finest 18th century landscape parks in Europe'. It was famous in its time and visitors could hire little carriages, drawn by horses, to take them round the grounds. The garden was created by Charles Hamilton who transformed a piece of Surrey heathland into an ornamental pleasure ground with an area of open parkland which predates 'Capability' Brown with its natural groupings of clumps of trees. Interspersed amongst these are temples, a lake filled by a great water-wheel designed by Hamilton himself, bridges and this grotto. Hamilton was also a pioneer in his planting of the new 'exotics', such as rhododendrons and other colourful species alongside native English trees.

BLENHEIM PALACE, *Oxfordshire*

Here 'Capability' Brown swept away much of Vanbrugh's layout. He raised the level of the lake, half submerging Vanbrugh's bridge in the process, and created a vast landscape, dotted with clumps of trees, laid out, it is said, to represent the battle of Blenheim itself.

ROUSHAM, *Oxfordshire*

The garden at Rousham has remained virtuall untouched since William Kent completed it around 1740. It contains all the essential ingredients, including a number of water features, temples and statuary, and views acros the River Cherwell to the open countryside.

WEST WYCOMBE PARK,
Buckinghamshire

The garden was begun around 1735 when a formal avenue was created and the stream was dammed to form a great lake. At that time the garden included a fort and a fleet of four ships was kept on the lake for mock battles to entertain visitors. Later in the century, Thomas Cook, a pupil of 'Capability' Brown, worked here, softening the straight lines of the earlier layout and introducing new temples, one, the Music Temple, on an island in the lake. Cook was followed by Humphry Repton who removed some of the earlier buildings and thinned out the trees. Little has been done since and what we see today is much as it was at the end of the 18th century, a perfect landscape garden.

PRIOR PARK, *Somerset*

Ralph Allen who had reorganised the country's postal system, made a second fortune from the quarries which supplied Bath with the stone which created much of that city's Georgian splendour. His mansion, at the head of a steep valley, overlooks the city. Alexander Pope was a friend and he created a 'Wilderness Garden' with winding paths, a grotto, and a sham bridge.

SHUGBOROUGH, *Staffordshire*

Thomas Arson (1695-1773), the brother of George, the famous admiral, inherited the Shugborough estate, bought up large areas of the surrounding land and demolished the village in order to carry out his grand designs. The landscape is undulating and depends for its effectiveness on water, trees and buildings. The first of these reflected the contemporary fascination with China, and a Chinese house was built to house the treasures the Admiral brought back from Canton. However, as the garden developed, the inspiration changed. Anson knew James Stuart who had published his 'Antiquities of Athens' in 1762 and commissioned him to recreate an Athenian landscape at Shugborough. So Greek architecture also came to adorn the park and this Arch of Hadrian is a copy of the original.

BRAMHAM PARK, *West Yorkshire*
This garden would have been rather old-
fashioned by the time it was completed in
the mid-18th century with its formal pattern
of alleyways bounded by high beech hedges
and geometric pools. A visit is an
opportunity to see an English garden in the
formal style before the passion for more
natural landscapes got into its stride.

STUDLEY ROYAL, *North Yorkshire*
John Aislabie, Chancellor of the Exchequer,
was disgraced by his part in the South Sea
Bubble scandal of 1720. Banned from public
office he retreated to Yorkshire and laid out a
garden on the hillside above Fountains
Abbey. The Temple of Piety is almost the
last classical building the visitor sees before
the great monastic ruins are revealed.

STOWE LANDSCAPE GARDENS, *Buckinghamshire*

Stowe was one of the earliest landscape gardens. It was originally designed by Charles Bridgeman, an early exponent of the new style, and William Kent, who here created the 'Elysian Fields', the gardens of the blessed, about which the Roman poet Virgil had written. The buildings have an explicit political message. The porticoed Temple of Concord and Victory and the curved Temple of British Worthies celebrate the democratic virtues of Greece and the liberties of the English constitution. 'Capability' Brown, who was on the staff, learned much of his craft here. He became head gardner in 1741.

HESTERCOMBE, *Somerset*

Hestercombe's landscape garden was the creation of owner Coplestone Warre in the early 18th century. By the 1970s all was derelict but since then meticulous restoration has brought the valley garden back to life. Restored buildings include the arched Mausoleum, Doric Temple and Witch House.

CLAREMONT, *Surrey*

Vanbrugh's original formal garden was swept away for a more natural landscape first by Kent and then by 'Capability' Brown. Progressive restoration has revealed just how important the garden was. The turf amphitheatre, designed by Charles Bridgeman, is a significant survival.

VIRGINIA WATER, *Surrey*

Water is important in landscape gardens
and a lake is almost always a central feature,
the still waters reflecting the surrounding
plantings and buildings. Fountains and
cascades provided the opportunity to include
contrasting dramatic elements and were
often powered by ingenious mechanisms
to ensure a continuous water supply.

SHEFFIELD PARK, *East Sussex*

Humphry Repton was invited to redesign
Sheffield Park, previously worked on by
'Capability' Brown. Repton was famous for
his 'Red Books' – collections of illustrations
showing patrons' gardens as they existed and
then, by means of overlays, how they would
look when his designs had been executed.
However, Sheffield Park remains largely the
work of Brown, but with massive colourful
replanting in the early 20th century.

FARNBOROUGH PARK, *Warwickshire*

While the philosophy was to work with nature, the new gardens were often themselves considerable works of engineering. Hills were smoothed out or enlarged, streams were dammed and mature trees were raised in large-scale nurseries and transplanted strategically to create the right effect. Buildings were hidden in the planting or terminated long vistas, height enabled a view to be created through the trees and the 'ha-ha', a sunken ditch and fence, made it appear that there was no obstacle between the garden and wider landscape. Created in 1751, the ambitious, three-quarters-of-a-mile, Terrace Walk at Farnborough, rises up from the house to follow the contours of the hill and has fine panoramic views over the surrounding countryside. An obelisk terminates the Walk.

MOUNT EDGCUMBE, *Cornwall*

The garden here dates from the mid-17th century, when there was much planting of trees as part of a national drive to grow timber for shipbuilding. In the 18th century the gardens became less formal with a 'Gothic' seat, an Ionic temple and these 'ruins', and views opened up to the sea and across the Tamar estuary.

GIBSIDE, *County Durham*

Coal-mine owner, George Bowes, spent much of his profits on his park in the valley of the River Derwent. He employed Stephen Switzer, the earliest English landscape gardener whose writings on gardens were very influential. Switzer planned the grounds in the newly fashionable style, with serpentine walks though thick wooded slopes and a long vista to the chapel.

Published in Great Britain by J. Salmon Ltd., Sevenoaks, Kent TN13 1BB. Telephone 01732 452381. Email enquiries@jsalmon.co.uk.
Design by John Curtis. Text and photographs © John Curtis. All rights reserved. No part of this book may be produced, stored in a retrieval system or transmitted in any form or by any means without prior written permission of the publishers.
ISBN 1-84640-036-8   Printed in Slovenia © 2006 Photograph on page 16 by kind permission of His Grace, the Duke of Marlborough

Title page photograph: Rousham Park, *Oxfordshire*
Front cover photograph: Stourhead, *Wiltshire*.   Back cover photograph: Croome Park, *Worcestershire*